YOUR KNOWLEDGE HAS V.

Bibliographic information published by the German National Library:

The German National Library lists this publication in the National Bibliography; detailed bibliographic data are available on the Internet at http://dnb.dnb.de .

Imprint:

Copyright © 2018 GRIN Verlag
Print and binding: Books on Demand GmbH, Norderstedt Germany
ISBN: 9783346079459

This book at GRIN:

https://www.grin.com/document/455690

Mohamed Bangura

Sociology of Intellectual Property in Sierra Leone

GRIN Verlag

GRIN - Your knowledge has value

Since its foundation in 1998, GRIN has specialized in publishing academic texts by students, college teachers and other academics as e-book and printed book. The website www.grin.com is an ideal platform for presenting term papers, final papers, scientific essays, dissertations and specialist books.

Visit us on the internet:

http://www.grin.com/

http://www.facebook.com/grincom

http://www.twitter.com/grin_com

SOCIOLOGY OF INTELLECTUAL PROPERTY IN SIERRA LEONE

About the author

Mohamed Bangura is an alumnus of Fourah Bay College, University of Sierra Leone and Africa University, Mutare, Zimbabwe. A full- time lecturer one in the Department of Sociology, Fourah Bay College, University of Sierra Leone. He teaches and writes in the areas of Sociology of Religion, Social Stratification, Social Research, Industrial/Sociology of Development and Organisational Behaviour. Bangura is the author of Organisational Behaviour: A Sociological Perspective and A Sociological Acquisition: A Sierra Leone Paradigm and two books of poetry (Waves of a Raining Mind and A Gaze of the Heart).

CONTENTS

FOREWORD

Albeit the discipline of Intellectual Property is significantly institutionalised and contributes immensely to the social development of western democracies, it is relatively novel in Sierra Leone as it is struggling with the harsh realities of socioeconomic growth as evident in Sub-Saharan Africa, especially within the West Africa Sub Region.

This book deliberates on the level of awareness of students and teachers of intellectual property and its relation with computer software in higher institutions of learning. The book therefore investigates the impact that intellectual property has on the use of computer software in teaching in colleges and technical institutions in Sierra Leone.

It specifically focuses on the careful use of computer software tools such as power point, computer aided instructions, and simulation, among others, by teachers to make learning simple and qualitative for the improvement in students social understanding.

A further motive behind this book is the need to explore the extent of the knowledge that college lecturers and students have about intellectual property as it relates to computer software in Sierra Leone.

The social discourse obtained from field in the country gave it considerable value to readers and the depth of analysis that is invaluable in looking at some of the more difficult aspects of Intellectual Property.

The outcome of the book further reaffirms the view that computer software is a very useful instrument in aiding the process of teaching and learning in higher educational institutions that now assume a leading role in the social learning process.

Whatever the nuance may be, it is clear that sociology does have an impact on intellectual property as well does intellectual property has impact on the use of computer software. This social impact is dispensed through the learning experience of the students and the teachers instructional social dispensation. It was also revealed in encouraging manner that computer software is more protected under copyright than patent laws. Despite the fact that computer software seriously affects the teaching and social learning process of users in higher institutions in Sierra Leone, there have been a number of bottlenecks which tend to derail such experience.

As revealed in the book, the problems involve threat from power failure, and lack of easy understanding of the software, among others. At any rate, however, the book shows the sociology of intellectual property and computer software are two sides of similar social thought.

Isaac Lahai Lamin
Computer Software Researcher (SMBJ)
Freetown City Council
Sierra Leone

ACKNOWLEDGEMENTS

My unequivocal thanks to Professor Joseph Aruna Lawrence Kamara (Deputy Vice Chancellor, Fourah Bay College, University of Sierra Leone), Associate Professor Bola Owen Carew (Assistant Deputy Vice Chancellor and Principal, Fourah Bay College, University of Sierra Leone), Associate Professor Kargbo(Dean, Faculty of Arts, Fourah Bay College, University of Sierra Leone), Dr. Dante Alie Bendu (Dean, Faculty of Social Sciences and Law, Fourah Bay College, University of Sierra Leone), Dr. Alfred Abioseh Jarrett (former Head Department of Sociology and Social Work) and from whom I derived my fountain of inspiration to continue to do research in my intellectual field of endeavour. The completion of this book is a testimony of the good intention of these renowned researchers as the set out to produce.

Special thanks is extended to Dr. Ibrahim B. S. Sesay (Postgraduate coordinator sociology option Department of Sociology, Fourah Bay College, University of Sierra Leone) for his professional kindness, yet he could be cruelly critical if he felt it was necessary to save me from some sociological folly to which I had become attached. From this man I learned much on sociological subject matters in Sierra Leone.

Finally, I must however recognise the encouragement and support of Mr. Munda Rogers (Public Relations Officer, University of Sierra Leone), Mr Calvin Macualey (Human Resources, University of Sierra Leone) and I also express my sincere thanks to the entire senior and administrative staff of the University of Sierra Leone.

To my wife Maimuna Bah

CHAPTER ONE:
THE EVOLUTION

The use of computer software as an aid in teaching is crucial in today's intellectual property world where technology seems to dominate every aspect of human social interaction and intellectual activities. In many parts of the world, computer has been adopted as significant tool in facilitating and fast tracking the many social activities that human beings conducted. In educational institutions people who were trained in the use of computers were employed to conduct administrative tasks involving the computation of students grades or establishing standardised database of students through the application of software that were installed into the computer hardware. The inbuilt characteristics of the computer system, such as its high speed and large storage capability, achieved through the invention of the integrated circuitry component called chips, accuracy and consistency in executing commands, and its unique ability to store and retrieve information, made its relevance highly enviable.

Considering the significance of the computer, its use was then extended to the classroom where it was intended to aid teaching process. Since the functioning of the computer is made possible through the social interaction between the physical components called hardware and the non-physical components called software, efforts were stepped up in inventing a range of software. These softwares were then divided into two main categories, viz; system software and application software. The system software is a set of programmes that is used to control the hardware and software resources. It is the main social bridge between the hardware, software and the user. The operating system is a major type of system software without which the computer system can never function. It is the nerve center of the computer. The other type of system software is the utility software which is referred to as antivirus used primarily to track down and clean virus in the computer. The application software, on the other hand, are programmes made for performing specific tasks. They include Microsoft Word used to process documents, Microsoft Excel used to produce spread sheet, Microsoft Access for the designing of data base, Microsoft Power point used to carry out presentations, and Microsoft Publisher used to carry out desktop publishing. The Personal Computer (PC), which is used by only one person at a time, is an integrated and compact system that features all of the elements and which is widely used today. The personal computer uses the processor and memory as two intertwined components, with the processor likened only to the brain of human be, it organises and carries out instructions that come from either the user or the software.

Computer software then makes teaching very illustrative and practical and enhances the increased understanding of the individual. However, the effective use of computer software, like all products resulting from human creation, is determined to a greater extent by the crucial role of intellectual property law. Although varying views exist regarding the nature and dimension of intellectual property law especially when it involves computer software, it nevertheless serves as an important kind of property with irresistible reward.

Until recently, Intellectual Property was a subject that was limited to the western countries. Initially intellectual property was mainly dominated by specialists and those who produced intellectual property rights. However, a significant shift away from this trend was made when the subject was subsequently integrated into multilateral trading system while at the same time creating impact on a number of key policy issues. Hence, this significant development made intellectual property gain wide recognition and importance in the lives of people in society. Today, it covers both OECD and developing countries. Intellectual Property includes patents, trademarks, copyright, industrial designs, utility models, geographical indications, and trade secrets. The importance of intellectual property, especially its rights and aspects such as patents and copyright, influenced most intellectuals to discuss it in gatherings or through volumes of pages. It then subsequently became an important concern for policy makers in both developed and developing countries.

Intellectual property law at the international level began in earnest around the late 19th century with the formation in the 1880s of the Paris Convention.

Subsequently, the increasing realisation of the significance of Intellectual Property in the different fields of human endeavour resulted in its expansion to cover other domains such as computer software. It became necessary to amend the laws to cover these new areas, and to make them more useful and affordable to the vast number of people in various national and transnational societies. The use of computer software in aiding teaching then became a necessity although in Sierra Leone this is limited mostly to universities and few tertiary institutions. Presumably, Intellectual Property should form a protective framework of software that is used in the teaching field. It is for this reason that developing countries, under the Trade Related Aspect of Intellectual Property Rights(TRIPS), are required to protect software under copyright law and semiconductor designs under the sui generis system in accordance with articles 35-37.

The field of computer software is obviously elastic and prolific. However, on almost a weekly basis, new technologies are being created that provide potentially transformative and more inclusive ways to communicate, to teach and to learn. However, these possibilities are permitted

7

more essentially within the framework of intellectual property. And fortunately, such possibilities have been granted under the Trade Related Aspect of Intellectual Property (TRIPS) agreement. It opens a new window of opportunity for adopting computer software in the service of humanity with specific significance generated through a synergy with Intellectual Property protocols. This marriage is made possible through the official recognition of Intellectual Property law as a major outlet for ensuring that computer software is not only used to teach but also makes it possible for its secured guarantee and protection from undue alteration by unauthorised experts.

From this direction, it is observed that the salient concern about the protection of computer software prompt the issue of code ownership and the software that enhances the computer's functionality serves as a focal point of social inquiry.

Computer software is a set of rules and instructions that enhance the functionality of the computer's operating system. It is the actual instructions that the user gives the computer which in turn gives out the required result. This basic understanding of computer software underscores its significance in providing leverage for man's utility. Hence, computer software is seen as a necessary interface between the teacher and the student in the social learning environment. With the use of computer software, the student's creative and innovative intuition is clearly enhanced through his or her detachment from the traditional method of instructional abstraction. He or she indulges in the pleasure of visual and artistic experience, controlling his own learning process with the use of basic hardware tools such as the mouse and keyboard. In between this possibility, intellectual property law offers adequate guarantee for the use of variety of softwares that are legally protected.

Hence, computer software and Intellectual Property are important in ensuring that human activities and development are systematically realised especially in developing countries. Unfortunately though, while Intellectual Property has taken root in some countries in Africa, the situation of Sierra Leone is quite different. The first attempt to exploit the use of intellectual property law in Sierra Leone was the enactment of the Copyright Law at the period of independence which became a significant part of the 1961 constitution. Since then however, the copyright law which was supposed to guarantee the rights of inventors and creators against piracy, was not taken seriously. It only remained on paper, and could not benefit from the possibility of effective implementation and popularisation. The grand effect was that most creative works of individuals were not protected against undue exploitation by non owners, a situation that continued for about fifty years, from 1961-2011. Throughout those periods, individuals almost lost ownership of their creative materials or products, and for most of the time they suffered from severe cutbacks in terms of the financial reward that they should supposedly realise. As a result of the remotely backward state of the country at the time, and the fact that Sierra Leoneans demonstrated high sense of inward disposition and conceit, caring little about development in the external world, great and notable local artists were more interested in the pleasure that they derived from their arts than financial reward. Their creative ideas were primordially tuned to the sacred traditions and culture which conspicuously held them to ransom. This status quo squeezed them of the essence of seeking any legal means or framework, such as those provided by intellectual property law, which will increase their chance of being maximally rewarded with financial fortune.

With the glorification of black market system, a seemingly negative commercial outlet shook the national economy especially in the 70s and 80s, local creators of ideas and inventions were at the center of those who suffered most. In those periods too, the act of piracy was so glaringly conducted that it almost became institutionalised, resonating with the prevailing hiking corruption rate that wrecked unchecked havoc on the state. The situation

became more serious and utterly critical when the music industry grew and was popularized in the early 2000 through the efforts of notable Sierra Leoneans like Jimmy B and Steady Bongo. More and more local musicians emerged with a number of local albums appearing in the market. But the musicians could not realise the financial reward from the sale of their albums. Unlike in the distant past when musicians considered their art as end in itself, this crop of musicians was highly critical and sensitive to the emerging economic trend dictating the existence of the common man. And haven experienced their brothers in the Diaspora making great fortunes from their albums; they wasted no time in expressing a fulmination for a legal means to protect their interest in the music world.

The reason for this was high levels of piracy which still prevailed in the face of the outdated national laws. This situation heightened by the unprecedented pressure from the public especially the music industry and writers forced Parliament to get down to business. They closely examined the law and made amendments. Hence, by the end of 2011, the Copyright Act was passed in Parliament to provide for the protection of copyright in Sierra Leone and for other related matters. Thereafter, it was then officially and legally proved that the local music industry and writers are now protected against undue pirating of their materials with high economic reward. It also created a formal platform for addressing disputes relating to copyright violations in a range of activities that were hitherto vulnerable to pirates.

Significantly, the Copyright Act covers computer software especially with regards its unauthorised use irrespective of the fact that the technology came into Sierra Leone quite recently, and very little effort is made to exploit its use in teaching.

Intellectual Property Law as it relates to computer software, is therefore a very young and almost virgin tool in Sierra Leone. Most users especially within the educational institutions have little knowledge of the relevance of intellectual property law and its crucial role in protecting computer software.

Facing modernity

Since the attainment of independence, the Copyright Act was recognised and enshrined in the 1961 constitution. But from that period onwards, little or no attempt was made to ensure that it is fully implemented. This position was obviously precipitated by the fact that Intellectual Property as a separate field of discipline was not fully recognised by those who were in the academic and leadership circles. Most users especially within the educational institutions do not know much about intellectual property which may be attributed to the late appearance and use of computer software in Sierra Leone. Ironically though, and as evident in the state constitution, intellectual property was recognised as early as the period of the attainment of independence, way before the experience of the use of computers in the service of man; but today the use of computer seems to be more popularised than the knowledge of intellectual property law. This disparity has had a downward effect that undercuts the very use of computers in the world of academia.

The situation is made worse by the dearth of empirical data addressing intellectual property and the teaching of students through computer software. Generally, this social direction pays very little attention to the impact that Intellectual Property has on the use of computer software. Intellectual Property and its comparative trend with that of information technology considered graphics under the terminology of educational technology and how it can be used in teaching process to facilitate learning in Sierra Leone generally. This social position recognises the crucial role of intellectual property law in determining the significance of graphics software especially for instructional purposes. Information technology also utilises qualitative strategy as a basis of social analysis by using a sociological imagination.

The key discourse underlying Intellectual Property and the use of computer software created the level of Intellectual Property awareness among the lecturers and students at University and technical institutions in Sierra Leone. The point is, how often computer software or computer aided programme is used as a tool of teaching by lecturers? What are the implications of using computer software that is protected by intellectual property law? How effective is computer software in teaching in Sierra Leone?

Noting the value

A sociological discourse on Intellectual Property Law and Computer Software is important in several ways, especially in a society like Sierra Leone where the subject matter is relatively novel. It will create the requisite awareness and in depth understanding of the subject in the context of Sierra Leone.

Considering the move that has been taken by the government of Sierra Leone in legislating Intellectual Property laws, especially the repeal of the Copyright Act of 2011, is very crucial in serving as a window of information that will guide the process in the future. This is very important when one considers the fact that there is limited research on Intellectual Property and computer software in the Sierra Leone context.

Furthermore, it is expected to serve as important material for policy makers in Sierra Leone and elsewhere in providing a clear understanding of the issues and synergy between intellectual property law and the use of computer software in teaching. Significantly, much interest will be cultivated in the sociology of Intellectual Property and Computer Software.

It will further create the awareness for providing the legal framework for products that are now being locally produced. Although, as an instance, computer and other relevant software are not being created in Sierra Leone, the lead role of Musicians and Writers may soon be replicated in the arena of technology which will make the exploitation of intellectual property law very impelling.

It will add to the body of knowledge available on Intellectual Property and computer software and showcase a Sierra Leonean perspective on Intellectual Property and its impact on the use of computer software in teaching, and also reveal the position of the country in the light of the growing importance and adoption of Intellectual Property in developed and some developing countries in the West Africa Sub Region.

Finally, the production of this material will mean that the country is gradually joining the other countries in exploiting the values of Intellectual Property for the development of their nations. This is very crucial when one considers the fact that Intellectual Property aids in the process of ensuring that development takes place especially for developing countries. It is therefore expected that this work will be among the early works that project into the need for Intellectual Property in the development drive of the country which emerged from one of the brutal wars ever recorded in the world.

Setting the discourse

This discourse is delimited in diverse ways as it is designed to be focused in selected colleges and technical institutions in the Freetown Municipality. It specifically draws samples from a population of students and teachers at Fourah Bay College and the Institute of Public Administration and Management on the one hand, and IAMTEC and African Institute Technology Holdings(AITH) which represent technical institutions on the other. The uniqueness of this within a specific context makes it difficult to be replicated exactly in another context.

It is also important to note that an investigation of the use of computer software at higher level of the educational system biases the discourse in favour of students and lecturers excluding the wider crop of educationists at the lower rung of academia such as the secondary schools. It is this genre of sociologists that is identifying the educational and social condition of children in Sierra Leone that are missing a lot in information technology and communication.

The responses of participants may gives a reflections of, and confined the context of personal experiences in the use of computer software in teaching and learning in Sierra Leone. It exclusively reflects a confined knowledge of computer software in colleges and technical institutions.

The fact also exists that only students and lecturers' viewpoints are considered in investigating the social link between computer software and intellectual property law. It clearly excludes the wider and more critical views of policy makers and officials in government institutions such as the Ministry of Youths, Education and Sports which is responsible for coordinating and implementing all educational programmes in the country. These potential group of people are not only external to the current social discourse, but a great service to the information gathering process by providing relevant and state of the earth issues that help answer the social research questions so far indentified. Given the mixed method it is presumed that more qualitative techniques explored provides for a subjective social analysis.

The social restriction paradigm

Although the social concept of Intellectual Property is significant in many ways, it has been limited considerably both in the course of a social perspective and the focus of the subject matter. As the case may be, even though the model focuses exclusively on intellectual property and computer software in the social context of Sierra Leone. This focus accounts for a narrow treatment of the subject of intellectual property as an independent and broad discipline that cuts at the heart of development in Sierra Leone.

The lack of adequate empirical discourse in Sierra Leone on the subject of intellectual property law makes it very difficult for an extensive social examination of the subject matter. In addition, there is also serious difficulty in the social understanding of individuals who seem to have little or no knowledge of intellectual property law as significant social tool that protects computer software used in most teaching processes. The delimitation of the respondents, in view of the number and constituents, also poses serious problem to the development of the research instrument to be used.

This is limited by the fact that much time and resources are required for the conduction and completion of the social research processes. Considering the disadvantaged society with very little exposure to educational facilities, a broader examination of the subject would only worsen social situation.

The difficulty emanating from the lack of adequate empirical works on intellectual property and computer software in Sierra Leone poses serious problems to the discourse process, resulting in near incompletion of other line of discourse.

Conclusion

This has shown that intellectual property has gone through a long period of development. In those countries where the discipline has been fully established, it provides huge economic benefits to those who have ownership of the creative works. However, there are still serious problems associated with the use of intellectual property in protecting ideas or products especially when it relates to computer software. In this regard, this context has endeavoured to look at the key issue of the impact that intellectual property has on the use of computer software in teaching in colleges and technical institutions in Sierra Leone.

The next chapter proceeds with an intent to conceptualised Intellectual Property and computer software. This is done with close attention to the extent to which both concepts are used in the service of man in the classroom.

CHAPTER TWO:
CONCEPTUALISATION

Intellectual Property as a specialist discipline, throughout its long historical lineage, was affected by a wide range of discussions and shifting debates as to its nature and relevance in light of socioeconomic development of the state. Over time, evidence found in the literature shows that sustained scholastic efforts were stepped up to explore the nature and accurate changes of the discipline, and the theoretical basis in which it is grounded. This presupposes that special attention is required by the researcher to conduct an in-depth investigation of the subject of Intellectual Property and its synergy with computer software. This is especially relevant in the context of Sierra Leone where both concepts are relatively new experiences with their benefits steadily influencing human interest.

Thus, this sets out to explore these concepts with the aim of providing fresh perspective on both concepts, while weaving out, perhaps on a very thin veneer, the link between them. This approach is very crucial in the determination of the relevance of intellectual property and computer software to Sierra Leone. In this respect, the basic assumptions on which the chapter is based, such as the development potential that intellectual property carries, the crucial protection that it provides for computer software, among others, are brought out.

Generally, two strands of scholastic enquiry; theoretical and empirical frameworks can be discerned from this conceptulisation. The issues relating to the concepts in question are examined. By using this approach, the chapter contributes by not only adding fresh perspective to the debate that dominates the field of Intellectual Property, but transcends to a point of providing strong justification as to the extent of the impact that it has on computer software in light of the latter's use in teaching, anchoring it on the objectives set out in the preceding discourse.

Considering the growing potential of the domain of intellectual property, it is expected that universal theories that provide rational explanation of the nuance that offsets a comprehensive balance between conceptualisation and practice, are readily available. But this revealing evidence indicates the difficulty involved in borrowing theories from other disciplines in the social sciences, simply because of the fact that the threshold of Intellectual Property is froth with diverging views and conceptions as to the dividing line between what to protect, and at what point should such protection take effect. While recognising the fact that theories of such nature do not provide a clear bridge between Intellectual Property law and computer software, this is squeezed along the path of placing the latter in the domain of laws of the former. It is the intention of this line of approach will aid in simplifying the confusion and perhaps unreliability of conceptualisations proffered, by establishing a link between the economic value of the impact that intellectual property law has on computer software and the technical considerations therein.

In view of the ambitious nature of this chapter, and the fact that the relation between intellectual property law and computer software is relatively novel in Sierra Leone, considerable attention is placed on the theoretical investigation influenced by the end economic reward that it has.

As much empirical research has not been conducted in the Sierra Leone context, especially with regards the impact of intellectual property on computer software, the chapter will be tilted heavily towards exploring experiences in countries where such awareness had long torched.

Theoretical Framework

The increase of human interest in intellectual property has influenced the emergence of theories focusing on the subject matter and its role in protecting ideas and products. The theoretical literature demonstrates series of opposing conceptualisations determined by the emergence of distinct ideological schools of thought. Exploring recent theories addressing intellectual property, noted that they are influenced by the struggles within four distinct approaches. One of the approaches is widely rooted in utilitarian tradition, which strikes a balance between the recognition of the originator's right to produce or increase invention and the public's right to its maximum utility. They Nevertheless, this emphasise the need for establishing a principle for the creator's recovery of his service and financial expenses incurred in the course of production as a way of circumventing widespread piracy through the granting of exclusive right to make copies of their creation for a limited period, and in the case of trade mark, be given the opportunity to explore and use wider range of vocabulary creating choice of trademark description that may attract consumers. While the utilitarian tradition generously makes provision for the inventor and consumer of products, this depends to a greater extent the right of the inventor with the concomitant effect of not harming the users or consumers of facts and concepts, which are held in common. Here, emphasis is placed on the inventor rather than that of the user. This fostered on similar premise that the owner of creative works should be entitled to some property rights that guarantee financial and other rewards as motivation to stir the creator's prolificacy, although it recognises the fact that labour is not involved especially in novel writings.

Generally, the complexity and sheer confusion that emanate from this application, especially concerning common property ownership create serious difficulty in its accurate application to the field of intellectual property. Theoretical projections highlighted are economic in nature, they nevertheless fail to provide universal framework for the straightforward understanding of intellectual property law in relation to authors' inventions. The same problem grips when an attempt is made to evaluate the impact of intellectual property on using computer software in teaching, especially in light of the volatile nature of the weak theoretical basis as evident in utilitarianism. However, an attempt is made to provide a rationale for resolving such fluid theoretical projections by evolving three basic approaches used in the applicability of those theories to intellectual property law and the improvement in social welfare. These include incentive theory, optimising patterns of productivity, and rivalrous invention. But even these approaches do not provide universal remedy, as they in themselves reflect similar shortfalls.

Contrary to the utilitarian concept of intellectual property is the view held by the school of romanticism which lays emphasis on the authorship and invention enforcing the notion of the natural right of the author over his creative product. This romantic notion of the author's right of intellectual property is the author's property from his or her mental faculty with a pure sense of inventions. This created a dichotomy between utilitarianism's incentive notion and the romantic's authorship defense, an ideological social cleavage that continued to fan the flames of tension in the acceptability or rejection of intellectual property law for longer period.

Intellectual property is really not about possession, but about control, and that intellectual property should be seen as the real property as opposed to natural property which is an illusion. A radical and straightforward proposition is relevant in the understanding of the relation between intellectual property and computer software. If intellectual property law is made to enable control over its use, especially with regards its patentability and copyright status, the better will it offer the opportunity for quality teaching of Intellectual Property itself. The reason is that the incidence of computer software pirating is higher today than any kind of property, especially in Sierra Leone where the law is best experienced on paper rather than in practice; but its wide use is often determined by the social status it does carry under intellectual property law than otherwise.

While the social landscape of intellectual property is inherently dominated by conflicting notions, and indeed counteracting scholastic responses, the central issue of the impact that Intellectual Property has on computer software and its use in teaching Intellectual Property is almost glossed over. Neither the utilitarian nor the romantics have been able to proffer satisfactory and all inclusive remedy to the problem.

Perhaps the realists' perception, for their direct handling of the issue, may have readily offered the domain of intellectual property and computer software with the right theoretical basis that will aid to underscore the Intellectual Property and computer software linkage. The note of realism's state-centric disposition provides its shortcoming as private actors, who have often forced changes in intellectual property protections, are overlooked thereby making it less relevant. On the other hand, functionalism at a face value provides justification for intellectual property law on the grounds that it enlivens efficient socio-economic relations especially in the context of the state. It provides explanation from contesting forces and interests as having provided rational settlements for the growth of the national economy. However, despite such macro perspective offered by functionalism, and the realists, it does not make adequate room for micro or non state private role in the intellectual property social philosophy.

The negative effect of all these conceptual shortfalls is that it leaves us in a state of suspended dilemma with an exposition to another difficulty which readily awaits us. The most obvious of this difficulty is the question as to what intellectual property is intended to achieve. Considering the scarce account of intellectuals on the impact that intellectual property has on computer software use in teaching, a further difficulty arises, which may not be remedied by merely relying on the available social discourse. This involves the efficiency side of computer software use taking into cognizance the prevailing situation in developing countries especially Sierra Leone. But before wrestling with this point, it is obvious that the question of the purpose of intellectual property in the light of its impact on computer software is addressed through the consequentialist justification which lays claim on the right that the inventor should have to reproduce and widely distribute invented work. In this way, the inventor's ability to reproduce and sell invented work en masse consequently benefits the public through cultural enrichment and improved quality of life. Thus in either way, both the creator and consumer benefit in the process, while the former is enticed to further productive spirit. However, the primary rationale for intellectual property is to protect inventions which include computer software in no small measure. By establishing such protection, intellectual property helps in ensuring that computer software, like all creations, is placed within the appropriate legal framework for its reliable use in the teaching process.

The complexity arises however in the qualitative nature of the impact that intellectual property creates. For a long period, this question of efficiency has been contemplated as a way of providing more technical and qualitative approach in teaching intellectual property as a specialist discipline through sophisticated software. It borders on the social question as to how often computer software or computer aided programme is used as a tool of teaching by teachers and lecturers?

It is important to note that computer software is very crucial in the teaching process. Its protection through patent and copyright creates a lot of possibilities and opportunities for the beneficiaries. It provides very significant uses to which computer software can be put in enabling teachers to effectively and frequently teach intellectual property to students. However, three basic softwares are often used in teaching, such as drill-and-practice software, tutorial, and simulation software, which maintain an increasing usefulness that makes teachers and students to use them frequently. For instance, computer software makes teaching very interesting and increases the learner's comprehension especially through simulation, and in helping the teacher with the many paper works such as marking of exam scripts. It also increases library use. Thus, this shows the essence and rationale for using computer software in teaching. However, present an existence of the impact that intellectual property has on using computer for teaching. This crucial aspect of the link between intellectual property and computer software is only, but often latently, addressed through theoretical social discourse. For instance, and as noted inter alia, the existing theories only labour on the point that computer software, like all other creations, needs to be protected by intellectual property law.

The use of Computer Software in Teaching in Sierra Leone

While social discourse provides wider basis for the understanding of the impact that intellectual property has on computer software, it does indicate the extent of the use of computer software especially in Sierra Leone, provides holistic answers.

It is worth noting that this domain draws extensively from the existing theoretical frameworks that underscore intellectual property scholarship and its need to be used in protecting computer software. From this angle, tries to provide answers to the questions as to the extent to which computer software is used in teaching in Sierra Leone.

The most obvious is the protection that it offers for the interest of the public that is the primary users, which prompts the development of more effective software including alternative types and affordability in terms of its use. In this vein too, computer software protection is not only limited to copyright law, but also that of patent law which makes it more efficient and adequate. One will not pause even for a moment to try to address the issue of the impact of intellectual property on computer software without examining those issues that are contingent upon it. Hence, several empirical or research questions deserve attention here. For instance, what is the level of Intellectual Property awareness among the lecturers and students at university in Sierra Leone? How effective is computer software in teaching in Sierra Leone? And, what are the implications for using computer software that is protected by intellectual property law?

While these questions form the basis from which to proceed, it to the realisation of its most obvious deficit; that very little, if any, research work is available which addresses intellectual property and computer software in Sierra Leone. However, the essentials of computer graphics in educational technology explores the significant role that computer graphics plays in the delivery of quality education to students in colleges. Specifically, it addresses the most significant question which torches on the central theme of concerning the factor that makes computer to be an effective teaching or learning tool, and the reason that makes computers to become teachers. There are four major reasons for the effectiveness of computers in education. These reasons include learning satisfaction, support for both teachers and learners, support for all content areas, and support for all age, grades, and all skill levels. Along these reasons, a striking element comes out glaringly, that the computer is capable of providing expert knowledge in anything and everything as long as the right kind of software is chosen and loaded into the user's computer system aided by an effective world-wide web access. This then highlights four major categories of software graphics commonly used by designers. These include Paint Software or Programs, Photo-Manipulation Software, Computer-Aided Design (CAD) Software, and 3D Modeling and Animation Software. To this list however, the use of Power point programme as part of office software can be added, as it is specifically used by teachers especially in the CISCO networking course offered at the Institute of Public Administration and Management. Thus, these softwares are the very tools used by the teacher or lecturer in teaching in the classroom. They make teaching very interesting to the students who experience the learning process as an artistic and social exercise. Through the use of graphics, such as images or pictures, as well as simulation techniques, the teacher allows the computer to do the actions while the students directly participate in the process. In this way, the social environment within which the lecturers and students operate in the classroom appears more friendly and familiar.

Perhaps the use of charts such as pie charts, bar charts, scatter diagrams, histograms, line and area graphs and a host of similar tools by a variety of softwares, give the computer the power to instruct in a way that makes learning a simple task. Not only is it that computer softwares enhance teaching through images and writings, most even have in-built speech features. They are mostly delivered on a one-to-one basis with an effect not rivaling that of the teacher. Considering the wide and complex nature of computer software especially as an instructional tool, it should be given due protection in a way that its effectiveness can be further enhanced.

The repealed Copy Right Act, 2011, provides adequate ground for the understanding of intellectual property especially with regards the protection of software and other inventions. However, computer software is found to be widely appealing to the teachers especially in providing the opportunity for dramatising history, which may also include history of intellectual property and its evolving theories. Thus, it is noted that computer software is widely used in such situation. The valuable works that incorporate copyrighted works may hamper the use of the material for teaching.

Conclusion

In the first place, the conceptualisation discourses provides divergent views regarding the protection of computer software by intellectual property law. However, there is high tendency of a consensus regarding such protection which with relative advantage for both the creator and consumers. There is very little research work regarding the use of computer software in teaching intellectual property especially in Sierra Leone. This situation is contingent on the fact that very little awareness exists concerning intellectual property and computer software.

CHAPTER THREE:
APPROACHING THE CONCEPTS

In approaching the concepts on intellectual property and the use of computer software in teaching, this approach creates a wide range of opportunity in the discussion since it enables one to direct a descriptive analysis or the qualitative question of "how" which is crucial in the understanding of intellectual property and the use of computer software.

Hence, what is examined in this include the case perspective, the why direction, the conservative matrix, the enveloped tool and the drive of the metropolis. These discussions are contingent on each other in a flexible continuum which makes it possible for the coordinated and sequential analysis of the concepts with a degree of precision.

A Case Perspective

This perspective is case a construction which covers Sierra Leone, with specific reference to Freetown, the capital city. It is lodged in order to thoroughly address the issue of the use of computer software in Sierra Leone. It also creates the opportunity to examine the relationship between computer software and intellectual property. It quantifies the sociological impact that intellectual property has on computer software and its use in teaching.

Both teachers and students found in colleges and technical institutions in Freetown are the main focus of this case perspective especially those who are exposed to the use of computer software as an instrument of teaching and learning from the close of the rebel war on to the repeal of the Copyright Act.

The Why Direction

Freetown which is noted for its population density and a centre of national administration. As a capital city, the use of computer by people for various purposes was first experienced here than in any part of the country. Also, the impact of the idea of intellectual property, especially the recently repealed Copyright Law, is clearly felt in Freetown than in the provinces.

Although the use of computer by Sierra Leoneans may appear to be widespread, its introduction in the country is relatively recent when one considers the experience in other countries in Africa and perhaps Europe. The use of computer was popularised especially after the end of the ten-year civil war which engulfed the entire country with a devastating effect. Before this period, computer system was considered as a sacred and highly delicate object that could easily be fragmented if not properly handled like an egg. Its possession was exclusively limited to the wealthy class of people who did not have much time for its use.

The idea of intellectual property was even novel than computer itself. Although the laws governing the ownership and rights of the inventor's ideas was codified in the country's constitution, an event that was effected in 1961 immediately after the country got her independence from the British, its true essence was never realised by the Sierra Leone population. For a long period of time, about fourty and more years, the laws dealing with intellectual property, especially the Copyright Act, only decorated a small portion of the national constitution. In those ugly years, then, computer software use in teaching was placed outside of the thoughts of teachers and stakeholders, especially the Ministry of Education at the time.

The early use of computer system by a small number of Sierra Leoneans was highly limited, intended for mere storage of the owner's personal documents. Hence throughout those periods, the state officials clued to the archaic use of filing system as a convenient, though crude, means of record keeping.

If computers were scarcely placed at the service of man in almost every sphere of state and public life, the idea of the use of specific software for teaching purpose was even too remote. The country was not advanced to catch up with the developed nations in taking full advantage of the technological evolution. Sierra Leone was almost cut off from the rest of the world in terms of technological engineering. The traditional blackboard teaching method was the only means of transmitting knowledge from the tutor to the student.

Given this circumstance, it was clear then that the significance of intellectual property was not being realised. Worse still, the consideration that computer software, and perhaps all forms of inventions, can be safely protected by intellectual property law was even untenable. As a result, the benefits emanating from the use of intellectual property laws to both the inventors and the users, as advocated by the utilitarian theorists, were not realised.

While this situation continued for as long as possible, a radical shift started taking place after the experience of the Sierra Leone brutish civil war. In the aftermath of the war, an intensive focus was placed on the need for Sierra Leoneans to acquire skills in computing as a means of becoming self reliant. The initiative was packaged in the disarmament, demobilisation and reintegration programme which targeted especially those people who had played active role in the civil war, and had become completely traumatised, and war weary. Through series of centers across the country they were thought in the use of computer software packages, and other skill.

This situation clearly laid the foundation for the use of computer software in teaching and the essence of intellectual property in facilitating the process. Hence, it was at the close of 2011 that the Copyright law was passed as a result of public pressure especially from the music industry in their fight against piracy. It made pirating of copyright works by unauthorised persons illegal and criminal and therefore punishable by law.

The Conservative Matrix

Generally, the teachers and students in key institutions of learning constitute the matrix, so to speak. Although the use of computer software is not restricted to only teachers and students, they are however presumed to be the primary users especially in the field of academia in light of the significance that it provides for them. Computer software, especially Computer Aided Instruction (CAI) such as simulation, is very instrumental in enabling teachers to teach in colleges and universities with increased efficiency. Besides, this crop of individuals is likely to appreciate and popularise intellectual property law and the impact it has on the use of computer software in teaching.

Furthermore, in order to ascertain the nature, degree and dimension of intellectual property and computer software, the population is disaggregated into gender (male and female) in light of both teachers and students. This gender dimension of the population is very crucial as it resonates with the rising phenomenon of girl child education in Sierra Leone, an element that has been at play in the reconstruction process of the country which still battles with the vestiges of civil disorder. The decision as to the nature and constitution of the sample size is very instrumental and deliberate intended to capture the missing link between intellectual property and computer software particularly as it affects the social teaching process.

Looking at this conservative matrix, it is crucial to determine the exact logical position of this matrix. But for the purpose of this social discourse, the conservative matrix is referred to those teachers and students who have lived in Sierra Leone, especially in the capital city, within the post conflict governance era.

The Enveloped Tool

Within this enveloped tool, specific colleges and technical institutions are the main units of analysis in lieu of the use of computer software as a tool for teaching. Hence, this tool is segmented into two broad sections according to the presence of those institutions in this discourse. The area between Waterloo and Eastern Police in the east end of the city is considered as one section. The other section, enveloping both the central and western regions, stretches from Eastern Police to Malama in the extreme westerly flank of the city. Within these sections specific institutions are located as the social pillar in that perspective.

However, it is important to note that this demarcation is obviously not balanced from the point of view of the structural makeup as reflected in the type of infrastructures, the population density, the character and psyche of the population and perhaps the development works generally as instituted by the national government.

Fortunately, the fact this enveloped tool is disaggregated into the said sections makes it convenient to determine the degree of computer use as well as intellectual property awareness among teachers and students. The table below is a visual representation of this enveloped tool.

Enveloped tool			
	Teachers	Students	
1. Fourah Bay College and 2. IPAM	20	20	
1. Institute of Administration, Management and Technology(IAMTECH) 2. African Institute of Technology (AITH)	20	20	
TOTAL	40	40	80

Field Survey, 2012

The selection of the sample above was done with one major goal in mind that is to ensure that it is structurally represented. This implies that the sample should comprise of a sufficient amount of respondents who represent the educational social structure and the phenomena in question.

The Drive of the Metropolis

In Freetown, the use of computer has been very common among students and teachers. It is clear that the rate of teachers and students using computers in the post Ebola period has increased. Although it has been said that the advent of computers in Sierra Leone is relatively new, its impact in the lives of majority of people is quite revealing. Among teachers and students in the colleges and technical institutions, such importance proves to be greater especially in aiding them both to teach and to acquire knowledge. Sierra Leone is least placed on the technological map in Africa way below Ghana, Nigeria and countries in the West Africa sub region, there is fair amount of optimism that soon Sierra Leoneans will catch up with others. What is missing however is the fact that the law that ensures the protection of computer software is not being enforced and that people are not made to understand that the unauthorised use of software, whether through computer systems or not, will be subject to punishment by law. At whatever rate, the awareness that computer software is protected under certain aspects of intellectual property law remains a reality, although such protection is only made under copyright. For instance, one school of thought believe that under the laws of Sierra Leone copyright is the only intellectual property law used to protect computer software in Sierra Leone. Hence, the other school agreed that computer software is protected more under the Copyright Act 2011, as against those who believe that it is protected under patent law as well. What this argument points at is that in some way computer software enjoys some amount of protection in Sierra Leone although such protection is not being widely recognised as a result of the fact that the existing law on copyright only remains nominal.

Challenges

Although there has been immense positive social impact of the use of computer software that is protected by intellectual property in teaching, it has not escaped its own problems which are as replete as one can imagine. The commonest problems that are often experienced by teachers and students in colleges and technical institutions in Freetown.Among these include the lack of computer software use in the event of power failure, the difficulty to easily understand the software, and that it makes teachers become bored especially when using drill-and-practice software. Other problems include the way in which computer software affects teaching trend in the event of faults and the view that it makes teachers become lazy.

In similar vein, students are also affected, especially in the course of learning. The lack of continuous access to computer by each student and the fact that they become bored as a result of the repetition that the software does in the course of teaching. It also does not create the pure social impact that the teacher makes in teaching, while it hampers students learning process in the event of power failure. It also affects students eyesight that relegates effective social interaction.

Conclusion

Intellectual property impacts on computer software in the course of a learning process. While quality teaching and learning is derived from the use of computer software, it also creates a social friendly and interesting environment for both the teacher and student. However, these problems pose a big threat to the learning process. But such problems do not undercut the significance that computer software offers.

CHAPTER FOUR:
SOCIAL IMPLICATIONS

The social implication in this direction based on investigating the problem of the lack of effective protection of computer software and other inventions which has resulted, though partially, in the low level of development. It covers the issue of the lack of recognition of intellectual property as an independent discipline in its own right.

Generally, intellectual property has become a separate field that is widely lodged on the socio-economic development of the country in diverse ways. It is emphasised that intellectual property law plays a crucial role in the use of computer softwares by teachers and students in teaching and learning respectively.

Specifically, it considers intellectual property as a powerful tool in protecting computer softwares that are used in the teaching process.

Intellectual property law in Sierra Leone saw a very significant step in November 2011 when the Copyright Act was enacted and gazetted as law. This significant step provides opportunity for the protection of computer software and other kinds of properties, as well as the increase awareness of intellectual property law as it relates to the ordinary Sierra Leoneans.

Conclusion

Generally, a discourse of intellectual property and computer software in a context where the use of both instruments are still new and, make it very difficult for a sociological attitude to explore effectively the problem being investigated. In the case of Sierra Leone, intellectual property has been dormant both in terms of the knowledge that people had about it and its social impact. It is only quite recently in November 2011 that much attention was focused on the issue when mounting pressure was made by leading musicians and other members of the public in the fight against piracy.

With the repeal and passage of the Copyright Act of 2011, the government was able to open a new window of social and economic opportunity for Sierra Leoneans to further exploit the fruit of their labour by benefiting from what they produce. The idea of intellectual property has permeated institutions of higher knowledge in Sierra Leone, the possibility now exists that in subsequent years much impact will be created in the lives of academicians especially in elevating the process of teaching and learning.

Hence, the revival of intellectual property law at a time when Sierra Leone students have started pursuing knowledge in such discipline in the diaspora, means that the right path to progress and development is being constructed.

Carving the Future

The use of intellectual property in colleges and technical institutions has been marshalled by a barrage of problems which affect both teachers and students, it is impelling that solutions are sought as a way of straightening the rough edges. This consideration has ignited the need to carve out the future path which require for an urgent action by the relevant authorities both from the social structures and institutions of government and the institutions of higher learning.

The impact of intellectual property law to be effected in lieu of the process of teaching and learning in higher institutions requires the need for a robust and substantive tutoring of the use of computer software in teaching should be considered strongly. This assumes the form of a general campaign launched across Sierra Leone in colleges and technical institutions. The starting point at the schools and grass root level. The culture of using computer in a learning process made obvious and compulsory, and made stricter at higher level of academia.

The government and other non state actors encouraged to intervene in ensuring that they provide a large consignment of computers and laptops for school going pupils and perhaps students. The idea of one-child-one-computer should be translated into reality. This will make it possible for the realisation of the wide use of computers by ordinary Sierra Leoneans right at the onset of their educational journey. In the event of the free or cheap possession and use of computers, the long trek to the localisation of the use of intellectual property law in protecting computer software will be driven to a road post.

While the availability of computers for the wide use of scholars is important as a solution, it should be accompanied by the supply of software that enables effective teaching and learning process to take place especially in colleges and technical institutions. Specifically, software that is less sophisticated should form the first point of trial in this all important business of intellectual property.

Furthermore, there should be the need for the wide use of intellectual property law in addressing the problem of piracy and other unauthorised use of inventors products and ideas by people for their personal gratification. In this regard, Parliament, the Judiciary, and the Executive arm of government should pull together their efforts in ensuring that these steps do not remain on paper. An enviable starting point is the organisation of fora which should involve the wider spectrum of the public with school going pupils, students and teachers taking the lead.

With regards the need to raise awareness about the essence of intellectual property, the gazette produced by Parliament should be widely circulated to the public and in higher institutions of learning at affordable cost. At the level of schools, it should be distributed on a free basis so that a wide range of pupils and teachers will possess them.

Perhaps the need for intellectual property law to be institutionalised in Sierra Leone will create a unique impact on the struggle to fine tune the use of intellectual property in protecting computer softer and other software. A special independent institute of intellectual property should be established under the purview and guardianship of qualified experts in the field to ensure that it is effectively managed.

Conclusively, for any serious and substantive approach to be used in ensuring that computer software, under the protection of intellectual property law, enhances teaching in colleges and technical institutions or in the country as a whole, then there should be the direct involvement of experts from other countries and universities where it has gained firm route. Since the hiring of experts may be costly, a further appeal should be launched to the international community and donor agencies to financially support the process. This support should involve both finances and equipments that are relevant to the establishment of intellectual property institutions and effective national computer system. Provision should be made also to train local Sierra Leoneans in the art of intellectual property and computer software so as to be able to integrate both fields in a most effective manner. It is only in this way that the long struggle to enhance the sociological impact of intellectual property on the use of computer software in teaching in Sierra Leone will be realised.

REFERENCES

Barrio, F. (2008). Learning Technologies as means and subject of IP Law Teaching.London Metropolitan Business School.

Baird, L. L. (1993). "Using research and theoretical models of graduate student progress. In L. Baird (Ed.), Increasing graduate student retention and degree attainment" in New Directions for Institutional Research 80. San Francisco, CA: Jossey-Bass Publishers. pp. 3-11.

Bessen, J., Meurer, Michael, J. (2005). "Lessons for Patent Policy From Empirical Research On Patent Litigation". Vol. 9:1.

Bitter, G.   G.   (1986). Computer   Literacy. Awareness.   Applications. Programming. Addison-Wesley Publishing Company, Inc. Canada.

Cox-George, N. A. (1961). Finance and Development in West Africa: The Sierra Leone Experience. London: D. Dobson.

Creswell, J. W., &Maitta, R. (2002). Qualitative research. In N. Salkind (Ed.), Handbook of research design and social measurement, pp. 143-184. Thousand Oaks,CA: Sage Publications.USA.

Creswell (2002). Quoted in Ivankova, Nataliya V. Students' Persistence in the University of Nebraska- Lincoln   Distributed Doctoral Program in Educational Administration: A Mixed Methods Study, December 2002.

Digital Media Project: The Digital Media Challenge: Obstacles to Educational Uses of Copyrighted Material in the Digital Age. A Foundational White Paper.

Drahos, P., Developing Countries and Intellectual Property Standardisation. IPRC Commission.

Dutfield, G. (2002). "Intellectual Property Rights and Development Policy Discussion Paper" UNCTAD/ICTSD.

Fisher, W. W. III (2007). When Should We Permit Differential Pricing of Information?

Gopalakrishnan, N. S. Course work on IPR and Computer Programme, Inter University Center for Intellectual Property Rights Study, India.

Handbook of Theory and Research, 11, pp. 90-136. New York, NY: Agathon Press.

Ivankova, Nataliya V. (2007). "A Sample Mixed Methods Dissertation Proposal".

Ivankova, Nataliya N.V. Greswell, J.W., and Stick, S. (2006). Using Mixed Methods sequential explanatory design: From Theory to Practice. Field Methods, 18 (1), 3-20 .

Main, Varda N. And Buehler, Marianne A. (2006): Intellectual Property in teaching and learning: Ownership, fair use and commercialisation. R.I.T. Libraries.

May, C. (September 15, 2006). Forgetting History is Not an Option! Intellectual Property, Public Policy and Economic Development in context. In Lancaster University, UK and Susan Sell George Washington University, USA.

Norton, P. (2001): "Essential Concepts (Fourth Edition)". Quoted in 'Essentials of Computer Graphics In Educational Technology' by Alhaji Usseif Sesay. Diploma Cultural Studies, B.A., Dip. Ed. (USL), October, 2008.

OECD/CERI International Conference Learning in the 21st Century (1998-2008). New MILLENIUM Learners: A Project in Progress Optimising Learning: Implications of Learning Science Research. Initial Findings on the effects of digital technologies on school-age learners centre for Educational Research and Innovation.

Okediji, R. L. (2004). "Development in the Information Age. Issues in the Regulation of Intellectual Poperty Rights, Computer Software and Electronic Commerce University of Minnesota, USA". Issue Paper No. 9 International Centre For Trade and Sustainable Development. (ICTSD) Geneva, Switzerland.

Rata, K. L. (April 27, 2011). "Executive Education Programs. WIPO Academy. Intellectual Property Education".

Samaddar, S. G. (2011). Teaching Quality Intellectual Property Management Using Information Technology in Indian Pedagogy. IACSIT Press, Singapore. India.

Story, A. (April, 2004). Intellectual Property and Computer Software. A Battle of Competing Use and Access Visions for Countries of the South, ITCSD and UNCTAD, Geneva, Switzerland.

Tashakkori, A., &Teddlie C. (2003). Hand book on Mixed Methods in the behavioural ad social sciences. Thousands Oaks. CA: Sage Publications.

Templeton, B. (2010). A Radical Theory of Intellectual Property. S.F. Publishing.

The Copyright Act (October, 2011). "Supplement to the Sierra Leone Gazette" VOL. CXLII No. 64. The Government Printing Department Sierra Leone.

YOUR KNOWLEDGE HAS VALUE

- We will publish your bachelor's and
  master's thesis, essays and papers

- Your own eBook and book -
  sold worldwide in all relevant shops

- Earn money with each sale

Upload your text at www.GRIN.com
and publish for free